novum pro

AF169163

ANGELICA FOMINA

FROM FEAR TO LOVE:

Transforming your relationship with money

novum pro

© 2025 novum publishing gmbh
Rathausgasse 73, A-7311 Neckenmarkt
office@novum-publishing.co.uk

ISBN 978-3-7116-0117-9
Editing: Vaughn Chambers
Cover photo:
Quietmind Art I Dreamstime.com
Cover design, layout & typesetting:
novum publishing

www.novum-publishing.co.uk

All rights of distribution, including via film, radio, and television, photomechanical reproduction, audio storage media, electronic data storage media, and the reprinting of portions of text, are reserved.

Printed in the European Union on environmentally friendly, chlorine- and acid-free paper.

ANNOTATION

We are accustomed to thinking that our knowledge, talents, and values will eventually translate into material wealth. However, real life doesn't always work that way. The amount of money in our account isn't determined by our abilities, mathematical knowledge, or even our moral qualities. A person's wealth is defined by how much they desire it themselves!

To attract money, you need to establish the right relationship with it. In this book, the author explains in detail how to do just that. It serves as a practical guide for implementing positive changes in your life.

This book will become a source of inspiration and knowledge that you will reread more than once.

TABLE OF CONTENTS

Annotation 5

Author's Note 9

Foreword 11

Chapter 1 13

Chapter 2 19

Chapter 3 23

Chapter 4 27

Chapter 5 32

Chapter 6 37

Chapter 7 41

Chapter 8 47

Chapter 9 55

Chapter 10 59

Chapter 11 63

AUTHOR'S NOTE

'Why are you poor? Because you're foolish. And why are you foolish? Because you're poor.' And it seems there's no way out of this cycle. 'There is a way out!' you might say, and you'd be right. But what is it?

Education, self-improvement, courses in personal development—all of these make us more educated, evolved individuals, but do they bring financial results? Why is it that spiritually developed individuals are often poor? This is a question that can be debated endlessly. People are as financially well-off as they want to be. The key moment is 'how much they want to be'.

Since the age of 13, I've been interested in questions such as, 'How was the world created?' and 'What is freedom?' (What kind of freedom or from whom? I myself did not understand.) The question 'What comes next?' interested me much more than 'What is happening now?' I've been working since I was 16, and I changed about 50 jobs (from a bakery to a production company organising international conferences, from KFC to an oil company, from an undocumented worker to the director of my own company) until I found what I liked.

The question 'Why aren't spiritually developed people wealthy, and is it true?' has occupied my mind for a very long time.

The answer to it is ambiguous. Many factors influence people's desire to be rich or poor. Their spiritual line also matters.

On the one hand, quest for a spiritual path may not prioritise wealth and they may choose other values such as harmony, peace, love, and balance between the inner and outer worlds. They may believe that true well-being depends not on the quantity of material possessions but on spiritual values, and thus, may not pursue money.

On the other hand, spiritually developed individuals may possess skills that aren't always related to making money. They may prefer work that brings spiritual fulfilment rather than a higher income, choosing growth over financial gain.

However, this doesn't mean that such individuals cannot be wealthy. On the contrary, they possess qualities that contribute to success in business, their career, investments, etc. For example, they may exhibit greater empathy, sociability, thoughtfulness for details, creativity, and more.

Thus, the connection between spiritual development and material wealth is not direct and depends on the individual values and abilities of each person.

It might seem that all your knowledge, talents, and values should eventually *return* as material wealth. But here's what's interesting: money isn't tied to moral qualities, mathematical knowledge, or other sciences. The presence of money in your life depends solely on your desire (or lack thereof) to have a relationship with it!

I've been planning to write this book for a long time. After realising that not having money requires a lot of effort, I understood that I was trying too hard. I tried my whole life when I could have just loved ... loved life, work, people, myself ... I realised that the amount of money depends solely on this love!

I offer you my map to wealth. It helped me. It will work out for you too, but it will require reading the book more than once. Moreover, it's really important to engage in the practical exercises that I'll provide here. Make some of them your habits, and enjoy the rest.

Wishing you an easy journey!

With love,
Angelique

FOREWORD

My dear reader, allow me to address you as such. You have decided once and for all to enter the realm of abundance and prosperity. Congratulations! Your time, your mindset, your relationships—all of these are in your hands. And this book will be the key to unlocking the source of your wealth!

All that remains for you to do is to apply the new knowledge in practice. But an important point: don't leave all the acquired knowledge at the level of theory, apply it. And the sooner, the better.

I know from personal experience what it's like to have debts, to live in fear of spending even a minimal amount on yourself, to work 20 hours a day, all while carrying a small child without any support.

Of course, one could argue: 'Who has it easy?' Everyone has their own pain, their own difficulties. But miraculously, when you talk to people about the good things in your life, they also remember the good things around them, haven't you noticed? When you complain to people, something negative automatically comes to their mind; conversely, when you talk about your good experiences, they automatically remember their own positive moments.

I stand for wealth for all, for abundance in every home. No one restricts us in this except ourselves. I'm sure you've heard and read something similar many times.

In this book, you will learn how to build a relationship with money and how to change these relationships, and understand what kind of relationships they can be. You'll grasp why we accept debts, how to get out of them, and what to do to rise to a higher level. We will undertake practical actions and acquaint ourselves with the rules that apply in the new era. In this book, I've tried to cover all aspects that influence money!

If you're tired of working as an employee, if you dream of having your own company but hesitate to start your own business, if you're stuck in a rut when you really want to travel but fear being left without means of subsistence ... then let's get to work! Start applying all the practical exercises described in this book.

And may there be prosperity in your wallet, on your bank cards, and everywhere you would like it to be!

Allow me to express my gratitude to my mentors—and also to my beloved man who has inspired and supported me.

I thank my family and my son!

Thank you, my dear readers, for your interest in this book and your readiness to build your future prosperity right now! I genuinely thank you for becoming abundant and wealthy, thank you for your future that starts right now. You're reading this book, which means you already have a desire to change your current state. I thank you for the future you are creating today.

Thank you, thank you, thank you!!!

And right away, here's your first practice.

Setting the Vibration of Wealth

Before sleep, repeat to yourself: 'Wealth and abundance.' Keep saying it until you fall asleep.

In the morning, you will emit the vibration of these words. Initiate this tuning process already tonight!

CHAPTER 1

The Speed of Money

Money is like those individuals who love speed. But to see them, you need to slow down!

The energy that attracts money, on the contrary, is very calm, viscous.

If you move very quickly, you simply won't be able to discern the money streams passing by you!

Why do I say that money has insane speed? Let's break it down.

When a person receives and spends money, they enter the realm of economics. If you love money or want to possess and use it, you need to understand that you are participating in the economy of a country (at the very least).

Economics is a primitive art.

Originally, the word *economics* meant the science or art of managing a household, and this remains its primary meaning to this day. Later, economics began to refer to the joint economic activity of members of society.

Money is the denominator of goods and services.

Have you ever wondered how many times we exchange *money–goods–money* in a single minute in the world? Imagine the turnover of all these transactions, purchases, and payments, and the speed at which they occur. Something is being paid for, bought, sold every second.

The speed of money is always much faster than yours, and if you can't train yourself, money will pass you by! Yes, you have to train everything, like muscles. Including money.

You can train yourself at any speed. It all depends on your production. No production, no speed, and no money.

Understand, this is a key factor that ensures speed and money in the economy. Money, in turn, is the result of selling goods and services. Without the production and sale of goods and services, companies cannot earn money, which can lead to financial problems and bankruptcy. Thus, production plays a crucial role in the economy and is necessary to create the speed of money.

The prosperity of any individual is directly proportional to the speed of the flow of their consciousness particles.

When your thoughts and your soul are on the same wavelength as your subconscious, you can control the speed of money and materialise any desire of yours. And in doing so, speed will not be something overwhelming for you!

For those who don't believe in the soul or the mind, I recommend starting by going to the gym. Work on your abdominal muscles until you get a six-pack and see at what speed you can achieve it.

The key point is as follows: do you confront yourself?

To confront means to face something, especially difficulties that need to be overcome.
To confront means the ability to be present and perceive comfortably, especially in the face of challenge, dislike, and accusation. (encyclopaedic dictionary, reference needed.)
To confront has nothing to do with confrontation.
To confront means to perceive with comfort, without experiencing a desire to avoid or evade. It is the manifestation of calm, non-tense attention.
The better you confront yourself, the more you can achieve.
The better you confront money, the more you can have!
It's commonly known that a person can never overcome challenges and obstacles by running away from them. You can't escape from money either, as it moves with enormous speed. And why run away when you can go towards it?

Therefore, the first step towards money, wealth, abundance, and your desires is the ability to face them head-on.

It's important to understand that there are rules of the *money flow race*, or, more familiarly put, the flow of money. In the past, in the previous matrix, or, to be more precise, before our transition into the Age of Aquarius, income was greater than expenditure. With the emergence of tools such as credit cards and overdrafts on regular accounts, the flows began to change. Very often, the outgoing flow exceeds the incoming flow, leading to debts (but more on that later).

The ability to take loans, on the one hand, provided opportunities. On the other hand, it mixed the flows and created a funnel. The number of tracks for different amounts of money to flow through led to an increase in energy on one side and the attachment of money on the other.

This is no longer just a flow; it's a specific, dense, distinct, independent, integral element of life.

Attempts are constantly made to simplify and make it less noticeable. Such actions lead to confusion.

I will explain later how confusion relates to money, but for now, let's examine what's happening in the new matrix.

You surely know about the elements, right? What about the elements? They are named just like the elements: fire, water, wood, metal, and earth.

We've learned to use fire, right?

Gas stoves, ovens, lighters. There was a time when we were afraid of fire.

How did we live before? That's a philosophical question, but the fact remains: we use fire and don't even think about it.

The same goes for water, wood, and other elements. Take any of the aforementioned elements, and its application will be self-evident to you.

So, money has become such an element.

The rules of using this element depend on your ability to create!

Yes! You can create as much money as you want! Until you do that, someone else is doing it for you, and that's why synchronising speeds is almost impossible.

Set yourself up for creation! We differ from each other in the number of desires, ambitions, talents, and those who allow themselves more, have more! Those who can confront more, have more.

It's worth thinking about this before we move on to discussing money relationships.

And how often do you come up with something? How often can you bring what you come up with to life?

You see, you need to create something so that it can be changed later.

Your salary doesn't come from some mysterious source. It's payment for your own production. Production is an action that yields a result.

I've always been amazed that people believe in *luck* as the only way to get rich and become powerful.

Luck is the option people usually resort to in that very state of confusion. When the forces they face seem insurmountable, they can always *rely on luck*. By *luck*, we mean *events that the person doesn't control*.

If someone lets go of the steering wheel of a car and hopes that, thanks to a fortunate combination of circumstances, the car will stay on the road rather than veering into a ditch, they're likely to be disappointed. The same thing happens in life. When you let something go with the flow, the likelihood that it will resolve itself is very small.

Perhaps you know how your friends, burdened with debts, grit their teeth and hope to win on the races to solve all their problems at once. Perhaps you know people who have been solving their life problems this way for years. The character Ebenezer Scrooge from Charles Dickens had a whole philosophy of waiting for the time when 'happiness would smile'. Yes, I admit, luck matters. But if a person has to rely on luck to cope with life, it means they're not in control anymore. It means they're in confusion.

Confusion can be defined as any set of factors or circumstances for which a solution cannot be found. A broader definition is: confusion is chaotic movement.

Confusion is when all particles of knowledge are in motion. It will remain so until no factor is defined or understood with complete clarity. Confusion is the main cause of stupidity. To a foolish person, everything except very simple things seems tangled.

Don't try to accelerate to the speed that's imposed on you; stop! You need to understand the speed (the amount of money) you can confront. And start with what you're sure about!

Certainty is the absence of confusion. Intelligence can deal with confusion. What are reliability and stability? The ability to navigate through confusion, navigate around an area of confusion, or bring order to it. Certainty, intelligence, and a sense of reliability and stability, can handle confusion.

And now, let's look at how luck relates to confusion.

Luck is the hope that some random event will help you in life. Relying on luck means giving up control.

Control can be *good* or *bad*, and the difference lies in certainty/uncertainty.

Good control is confident, positive, predictable control. Bad control is uncertain, variable, and unpredictable control. In bad control, there's never any certainty.

You can control the speed of the money flow if you don't chase after it. You can also create it and manage it!

Exercise
Rocking the Energy of Money Flows

Start keeping a diary of expenses and income for each day. Record every amount you spend and earn. If you're already maintaining such records, continue this practice. Write down the names of your favourite designers or brands. Then take a look at your favourite items and think about who created these things that we buy and use. Find the history of your favourite brand or product, such as your favourite ice cream or wine. Learn more about the creators and the origins of what you value.

Reflect on the question of what affects the speed of income. Write down your assumptions and possible answers. In the next chapter, you'll be able to compare your thoughts with the answers I'll provide.

Note: These exercises are aimed at actively engaging with the topic and stimulating reflections on money and money flows.

CHAPTER 2

A New Element in the New Matrix

To avoid confusion, you need to accept one fact. Money is a new element. The new era requires additional codes, and these codes are digital!

If it's difficult for you to accept this fact, you can consider money as an element of *metal*. Remember, in past centuries, coins were made of gold, copper, and silver. Or you can classify money as an element of *wood*, considering paper banknotes. Money today is not just a subgroup, it is an independent element! It exhibits all the characteristics of metal, wood, water, and even fire.

The emergence of digital currencies is direct evidence that a new element is integrated into the new matrix!

Let's take cryptocurrencies as an example. Do you know what's interesting? This currency has no government support anywhere! Only consumer demand influences the price of crypto. Crypto is essentially a digital code!

A new era has arrived; that's not a secret to anyone. Along with it, a new matrix has loaded!

The advent of high-speed internet, online payments, and cryptocurrencies – all these are signs of the onset of a new era.

New professions are emerging, and there are a lot of numbers around. Have you noticed that?

Do you think this just happened? It appeared, and we continue to live. Many find it very difficult to accept the new. Some people are annoyed by non-cash payments and settlements.

In reality, living in a new way is wonderful; you just have to accept it!

The times of burning people at the stake are over, and I'm very glad about that!

I actually wonder why wars are still fought using old methods. It's possible to wage war in a completely different way.

War is a threat to humanity because humans can't confront war. The idea is to make war so terrifying that no one will be able to fight anymore.

The invention of the longbow, gunpowder, heavy naval artillery, machine guns, hydrogen bombs only adds to humanity's confidence that war will continue forever. When all the new elements that a person can't confront are added to the elements they couldn't confront before, their ability to cope with war diminishes.

And what about your ability to confront money?

Let's return to our new era, our new reality for now. The matrix includes all the previous elements and the new ones. Money is one of the new elements that make up the new era!

If you think about it, in the past, exchanged items included seashells, stones, clay objects, leather, fur—essentially, things that were liked, things that were beautiful. I'm sure broken seashells didn't attract anyone. All these items served as a means of exchange. Later, semi-precious stones were used for adornments, and they weren't easy to obtain.

Cleverness and imagination were required to find something that could be used to buy other things. It had to be something remarkable, something different from the rest. And most importantly: other people really wanted to possess that thing. Do you understand what I'm talking about?

There's always a shortage of what others want. It creates scarcity, chaos, tension, competition.

To alleviate the tension and scarcity of money, they came up with bank cards. A very convenient invention, and the fact that there's overdraft completely undermines the significance of paper money. You don't have specific numbers in front of you like with cash, but there's a subconscious sense of an amount you can spend. Extra funds from the bank are quite relaxing; after all, you always want to buy something.

However, here's the catch—misusing funds leads to the poor becoming even poorer!

You see, exchange is simplified. Bartering, swapping goods for goods, cannot be objective; another element is needed in this equation. Money is the proposed element that everyone agrees upon. If you disagree, propose your own terms of exchange, why not? Money symbolises things. It's the denominator for goods and services, ideas and thoughts! And to make this exchange easier, concrete numbers have been replaced with cards (it's like there's money, but it's also like there isn't).

The speed of income is directly related to the speed of delivering and receiving results! There's your answer to the practical exercise above. Compare it with your notes.

The process of exchange is now significantly simplified. You use your card for transactions, and that's it. However, your card must have incoming funds. The simplest way is to obtain an overdraft or credit from a bank. But then, how do you repay it?

Income comes from the creation of a finite valuable product—something that can be shared with others and exchanged for support. A valuable product is valuable because it can potentially or actually be traded. The more you engage in exchanges, the faster your standard of living changes.

The concept of *standard of living* can be defined as the relative quality of a person's (or a group's) belongings, accommodations, food, equipment, and tools, as well as their conditions of work and existence. This also pertains to your environment.

The personal production of valuable finite products and the standard of living of those who produce them are closely interconnected. This is a fundamental law of economics. To maintain their standard of living, individuals must produce more than they require.

The foundation of a standard of living is a product. A product doesn't materialise out of thin air. It emerges through work that is genuinely carried out.

If you possess the ability to create a product, whether you realise it or not, you're engaging in exchange, and your card cannot be empty.

If a certain number of individuals within a group—such as your company or family—produce fewer products than necessary for sustenance, they diminish the standard of living for the entire group, company, or family. If some members of a family, group, or company not only fail to produce valuable products but also produce faulty ones, they actively lower the standard of living for each individual in that group or team. When a group has a very low standard of living, to understand the cause, it's necessary to examine where the disruptions occurred.

Frequently, many appoint themselves as *saviours*. However, you shouldn't elevate the standard of living for the entire group. Improve your work and gain more.

When society is flooded with irrational theories, violating this rule results in numerous negative examples. The wealthy, who genuinely work tirelessly, are often perceived as idlers or even frauds. Idleness is sometimes mistaken for the best lifestyle. An impression is created that someone is obligated to provide means of existence to a person without any effort on their part. You know, the most dangerous thing is to not demand production from others. Or to pay for services that don't bring any benefits. This principle operated in the previous matrix, and it operates in this one as well.

Practical Exercise
Elevating Your Standard of Living

Write down what you contribute to your group, family, or company.
What can you improve in your product or service, or what would you like to enhance?
Are you producing enough for your standard of living?

CHAPTER 3

The Energy that Influences Money

Let's consider these questions step by step. Many associate money with the concept of *energy*. This is very accurate. Energy is present in everything, including money. Energy is the foundation of all foundations, not just in the context of money. If you have financial problems, the root issue is likely somewhere entirely different.

Money and sex are the most corrupted energies in the world. Everything operates under the law of *survival*. Every cell, microorganism, and microbe in our Universe wants to live and, accordingly, adapts to new realities.

In matrices, there are their own codes, inscribed in their own language:

Energy (vibrations, rotations, sounds): the very first matrix consisted solely of energy.

Colours: the second matrix, because as the Universe ages, it contains more shades. Over time, colours were added to energy, representing the next stage of development and the loading of a new matrix.

Letters: The third matrix. It's the language of our subconscious. We encode our reality, thoughts, mentality, beliefs, and ancestral programs using this language. Energy and colours were no longer sufficient for encoding new programs, leading to the emergence of languages and the development of writing.

Now Numbers have been added. This is the fourth matrix, as monetary units default to becoming our life's code. There is a lot of information about the new dimension now; some call it a transition to the fourth dimension, others to the fifth. In reality, it's the addition of another code.

To cleanse the energy or what is also called the *first programming language* to its pristine state requires a lengthy and meticulous process. Establishing relationships with new elements is much simpler! By changing the rules of the previous matrix, which include beliefs, convictions, and family values regarding money, you can quickly, easily, and advantageously construct new relationships for yourself in the future.

You can change your life right now! You are what is reflected. How can you understand this? Look around and listen to what others tell you! Yes, there are many distortions, I agree, but there is still a significant portion of truth about you!

What do you hear?

When you hear *beautiful*, your subconscious is transmitting: you are beautiful. You might harbour doubts, but your code communicates this to those around you.

If you constantly hear that you are strong, it indicates your subconscious is transmitting precisely that.

Unpleasant opinions that you disagree with might also arise. In that case, rewrite your records, and others will read them without even realising. You will begin to live the way you truly desire, not dictated by your unconscious.

Your desire to *possess* is mainly influenced by the energy of your thought forms. Your actions follow your thoughts! If you perceive money as unattainable, in your reality, irrespective of your actions, you will lack money. They heed the command of *unattainability*.

Realise that your prohibitions have no bearing on money. Prohibitions are your inner issues! Let's revisit the first chapter and work on confronting them. The energy of your income depends solely on you, and its quantity depends on the number of people involved in your process.

Remember, to exchange something, you need to find demand for it or create such demand. Money is an *idea backed by confidence*.

The idea is that the direct bartering of goods or services is too inconvenient! Confidence arises because this monetary unit, this piece of metal, paper, or another form of money, will be accepted by others only after you accept it in exchange for what you desire to possess. Confidence also extends to the country that issues these currencies.

Practical Exercise
State of Abundance Awareness

Reflect on your ability to *transform*. Capture the state of complete abundance, where you can create what you desire from nothing. Conversely, experience the feeling of liberation when you are overwhelmed and you can let go of all that is unnecessary.
Imagine how all your desires materialise:
How is the material for your clothing produced?
How is your dream home constructed, and where do you obtain construction materials?
Perform this exercise without money. Mentally create chains of the creation of your desires. Consider how many people are involved in fulfilling your desires and how much energy is required.
Engage in this exercise as frequently as possible, paying attention to details. This exercise reveals your potential and enhances your creative ability.

Exercise
Money Beliefs

Divide a sheet of paper into two columns. Close your eyes and transport yourself back to your childhood. Recall a situation related to money. Listen to what your parents, grandparents, and you thought. Record everything in the left column.

Close your eyes again and transport yourself to your teenage years. Remember a situation involving money and record your parents', close people's, and friends' thoughts and words, along with your own.

Record whatever comes to mind. Close your eyes once more and return to the present, to a situation involving money. Write down your thoughts and the words of those around you—parents, spouse, colleagues.

Examine your beliefs once more and write them in the left column. In the right column, list new beliefs. Tear off the left side and read the right portion—your new positive affirmations—for 21 days. Create a new, brilliant, ironclad program for yourself. Write it now, incorporating your new beliefs, and seek confirmation in your life for another 21 days.

Apply the following steps in any sphere of life:

1. Define;
2. Modify;
3. Observe.

CHAPTER 4

Two Paths to Achieving Wealth

Wherever we are, whatever we read, poverty has always been undesirable for everyone. Wealth, luxury, beautiful expensive decorations have always been revered and sought after!

Poverty is abnormal, undesirable, and unattractive.

Wealth is normal, right, and fantastic!

Today, no one hesitates to ask: 'Where do you work?' or 'What do you do?' People want to assess the degree of your earnings to understand how much money you have. Sufficiency remains an indicator of many aspects of life. Money becomes a criterion for success.

Those who consider money evil are probably afraid of themselves. Is money good in and of itself? That is a question for you.

Remember, as in the fairy tale: 'They started to live and thrive, and to amass wealth.'

If you don't like and don't want money, don't be surprised when you don't have it. Remember: 'As you wish, by Pike's command?'

But for those who do love money and want more good for themselves, let's move on.

There are many ways to achieve wealth, but I will offer you two options:

Working on your money mindset.

Establishing new relationships with money.

Why am I suggesting these options? I use them myself every day and I see results every day. Those who practice working on their thought forms always have results from their efforts.

I want to say right away that in both cases, your beliefs will influence you. You will need to change them, erase them, replace them. But it's not as difficult as it might seem.

The first option is related to the previous matrix. If you have worked with your beliefs and don't see the desired results, then most likely:

There are more ancient settings, not necessarily related to money.

You've removed money programs but haven't installed new ones.

Your thoughts today do not allow you to *attract* the desired amount to yourself.

You lack self-belief.

If you audit yourself, your thoughts, your environment, you can look at/assess/understand what you have in your subconscious mind:

Do you like where you live?

How are you dressed?

What do you say and how do you say it?

Where do you work?

If your answers to these questions are more than one 'no', then think about why.

A good question, isn't it? Reread what has been said above again.

If you have never worked on your settings, it's time to start. Your thoughts are your reality!

Yes, it may sound banal, but everything you think, you have. Something isn't right? Change your thoughts.

If we assume that the body is a machine and the brain is a computer, then programs are our beliefs. Beliefs need to be worked on, recoded, tuned to a different setting ... It's simple!

Track what and how you think; write down all negative thoughts and phrases you hear or say yourself. Replace them with other phrases and beliefs; repeat this for at least 21 days, 108 times a day. That's it! New programs; a new setting is ready. You just have to observe the changes that will happen sooner or later. The speed of change will depend on the difference between the programs you deleted and the ones you installed. But I guarantee you: new settings will be reflected in your reality. If not immediately, then after a certain time for sure!

You can start with the second option, establishing new relationships, but still, you will have to learn how to work with settings. It's better to do it sooner, as then you will achieve the life of your dreams faster.

Once again, I want to return to the exchange.

You now know that you can change your programs. Notice, it's quite easy. Of course, it will take some time. And if you were offered to pay money for it, provided that the new programs would work immediately, would you pay for it? I would! For saving time, for the speed of changing life. To say more: I believe that would be an honest exchange!

Robbery. What? Yes, yes, this is a type of exchange where money is taken but nothing is provided in return. Such an exchange is practiced by thieves and other criminal elements.

Deception. Yes, my dear ones, this is also an exchange. When an order is accepted, payment is received, but the service is not provided fully or is of a lower quality than what was ordered. In such cases, debts arise, as the owed amount for services or goods keeps increasing.

Honest exchange. The order and the money are exactly as they were ordered. Most prosperous companies operate based on an *honest exchange*.

The last type of exchange is not very common. It can be called *Exchange in Abundance*. This doesn't mean providing services for free. It means offering something more valuable than what was received in exchange for money.

You might not believe me, but income depends on which of the four types of exchange mentioned above you engage in. This applies not only to organisations or groups of people but also to individuals. And not just in the workplace but also in everyday life.

In the first type of exchange, there will be no income. Many may have doubts about this, but the fact remains: robbers and fraudsters will not profit. At some point, they will face failure.

The second type of exchange sustains a group or an individual for a limited time only. In the end, there will be a painful loss of status or position, and income. Taking money and essentially not producing or delivering the promised goods or services is a path to inflation.

The third type—*honest exchange*—leads to a relatively stable situation. It is considered fair, acceptable in society, and lawful. However, it does not guarantee the expansion or development of a group, nor the well-being of an individual. It is not sufficient.

The fourth type of exchange is my favourite. Providing something in abundance and of higher quality than expected. And receiving payment for it. Doing your work better than expected.

Only a few use the fourth type of exchange, and it's a pity. This is the key to spectacular success.

This type of exchange works for both a company and an individual.

Let's return to wealth.

I hope you now understand that money does not depend on your beliefs or your love. But the quantity of money in your life depends on these concepts.

And wealth? The only wealth of a country is its natural resources, the willingness of its population to work, and the genius of its scientists.

For people, wealth is their personal happiness. Not the number of pounds, dollars, or roubles. A worker's wealth is their potential ability to work, create, love. This signifies their potential ability to get along with others, plus or minus another 30 years, during which you can work and interact with people. This is wealth!

I can add that wealth is measured by the number of friends, and the belief in one's ideas. This is true wealth. This is life! If a person can live with pounds in a bag, then for them, wealth is money. But can one live in a bag?

If you don't manipulate this, don't create confusion, then there are no problems. When disagreements arise in relationships, something is always amiss. This is how confusion, manipulation, and problems arise.

To confuse anyone, it is enough to find what they believe in, what they are confident in, and devalue it. To activate all the confusion that was once within a person, it is necessary to shake stable data, criticise them, or provide evidence against them.

What one person believes in might not be relevant to another. Everyone accepts what is closer and more understandable to them, and everything else is considered in line with that.

To get out of confusion, simply accept new data or restore old ones.

I hope you now understand what wealth is. Wealth is only as good as it is understood. Work is only as good as it brings pleasure, not how it is paid. Natural resources are only as good as they can be used, not discarded. And a thought is only as good as it can reflect a person's goals and desires. And all of this becomes wealth!

CHAPTER 5

How to Determine Your Relationship with Money

Money can be a wonderful intermediary that can work both in your favour and against you. It is a tool that has the potential to open any door. But there's a significant *but*. Obtaining this key is possible only through your own relationship with money!

So what does it mean to build a relationship with money? And how can you tell if you have a relationship with money?

Relationships with money are a complex and multifaceted process that encompasses not only our financial actions but also our emotions, thoughts, values, and beliefs. Below are some signs that you might have issues with money:

Stress and anxiety related to money. Worrying about bills, debts, lack of financial stability, etc.

Feelings of guilt and shame related to money. For instance, feeling bad about your debts or needing to ask others for help.

A lack of understanding of your finances and an inability to track your expenses and income.

A desire to spend beyond your means, leading to debt and loans.

Frequent conflicts in relationships, especially with your partner, about money matters.

A lack of financial stability and confidence in your financial decisions.

Lacking the ability to plan and pursue financial goals, such as savings, investments, or debt repayment.

Signs that you might not have a healthy relationship with money:

A lack of control over your income and expenses.

The absence of a *financial instinct*, so to speak.

The accumulation of debt that is difficult to get out of.

Business struggles or a stagnant income, difficulty finding a job.

The possession of material goods but no savings.

Generosity towards others but a reluctance to treat yourself.

Often spending all your money down to the last penny only to experience a sudden influx of money afterwards.

Accumulating a small amount of savings only to spend it all immediately due to unforeseen circumstances.

Understanding your relationship with money is crucial for achieving financial well-being. If you recognise any of these signs in your financial behaviour, it might be time to work on improving your relationship with money. Remember, building a healthy relationship with money involves not only improving your financial habits but also addressing your underlying beliefs and emotions related to money.

Is this available?

Then I can congratulate you—you don't have a relationship with money!

But you can create one.

Just like any other relationship, you can at least try!

If you've ever experienced failure in something, you probably don't want to go back to that experience. If something was taken away from you, stolen, you likely have a protective reaction. And since the subconscious mind contains much more information than we can analyse, we automatically resist repeating such events. This is the defence mechanism of past defeats.

If you don't have a relationship with money, it means you didn't want one. This unwillingness is concealed behind the protective mechanism of your subconscious mind. Accept the fact that we, as humans, have the right to failure, loss, mistakes. Allow yourself that. Having a relationship with money means as many times as you allow yourself!

Deciding once to build a relationship with money, you will achieve (I guarantee):

Safety and confidence in your relationships with your partner or friends regarding money, and the absence of frequent conflicts.

The ability to use money to achieve your goals and improve your life, without spending more than you have.

Practical Exercise
Basics of Financial Literacy

Write down what you need money for (list all your boldest desires and dreams, along with their costs).
Divide a sheet of paper in half. In the left column, write down your basic monthly expenses (housing, food, transportation). In the right column, list 10% of the total for five different additional budget components:
Untouchable reserve (you can even start with 20%, the more the better, but start with 10%).
Education.
Investments (to be accumulated and invested only after six amounts are saved in the *untouchable reserve* column).
Travel.
Additional expenses (this could include clothing, restaurant outings, hiring help around the house, etc.).
Calculate the sum of these two columns—this is the amount that determines your current standard of living.
Does this amount match your income?
What can you do to increase this amount?

Exercise
Forgiving Debts

Write down on a sheet of paper all the promises, commitments, and agreements you've made to other people! Start with clients and colleagues. Write down everything you can remember—writing a review, sending a link to a video, conducting a session, an event, a workshop, a live session, etc.

List all your *hanging* debts and obligations to other people. For those who want to go deeper, do the same thing, but with debts that have accumulated in your personal life (promises to your spouse, children, parents, friends, colleagues that you haven't fulfilled).

For those willing to delve into the deepest layers, list the promises you've made to yourself but haven't fulfilled yet. It might be painful, but the truth heals.

Next step, analyse your lists of promises! Start fulfilling them! You can do a small promise IMMEDIATELY! Right after reading this chapter.

Perhaps you'll realise that there are things you don't want to do, and you promised them to someone for no reason. Send a message or call the person you owe, even if they're no longer expecting anything. Honestly say that you won't be able to fulfil your promise. After the conversation, cross this promise off your list and out of your mind.

Continue working through your list of debts in this way; observe your feelings and energy levels. Record your insights and realisations.

How do deferred tasks and obligations affect finances?

Let's delve into this together. First, the feelings and thoughts about tasks that you promised to do but haven't completed.

What will happen if you ignore these tasks and obligations? These tasks remain *somewhere* with you. Gradually, you forget about them; it becomes difficult to remember who you promised what. Yet, the sense of duty remains and resonates in your life.

This feeling begins to shape a reality where there are debts. The simplest way to manifest debts is to incur financial debts!

In order for you to have debts, you need to either block your income (no clients, no salary, clients not paying for your work, no orders, etc.) or incur unforeseen expenses (car breaks down, laptop malfunctions, fines arrive, etc.). It might be a combination of both. Expenses have grown, income has disappeared ...

And now you are in debt. But now, the feeling of *I owe* and external circumstances are aligned! There is a debt on the account or a debt to other people. And they won't let you forget about it! People remind you that you owe them. The bank deducts money from your account for credit with interest.

To start getting out of this situation, I recommend starting with lists of unfinished tasks, in order to first see and recall the promises you made to other people and to yourself.

*Exercise provided by Nadezhda Kharitonova – a female coach, psychologist, constellator, theta practitioner, play practitioner, author, and leader of workshops.

CHAPTER 6

Potential Relationships with Money

A Bit of History on Why *Having* is Important.

In this context, *having* means the ability and desire to possess something, to buy with money, or simply to have financial accumulation.

Understanding our family history, our needs, life principles, how deeply we allow ourselves to philosophise—all of this influences our concept of *having*.

Attitudes towards money have varied across different countries. Each had its own money-related rituals.

Different social classes also had different attitudes towards money. These relationships are either encoded in our DNA or they're not.

Currently, these social classes still exist, and depending on the level we're at, we have a reciprocal relationship with monetary units!

In simpler terms, each profession has its own monetary framework.

If we want to earn more money, we need to perform our work better! The better we do it, the higher payment we can ask for.

Whether we have the courage for this is another question. This doesn't have a direct correlation with money.

Professions in the past without direct relationships with money:

Healers;
Military personnel;
Scientists;

Royal family members;
Priests.

Professions in previous matrices where financial connections were established:
Craftsmen;
Merchants;
Travelers.

The more representatives of these professions that exist in your lineage, the better your relationship with money is *programmed*.

Your personal history of past lives is more significant than the history of your lineage.

We have two lines of development:

Genetic, which is passed down through the lineage. This is cellular memory determined by our DNA from each ancestral tree.

Spiritual. If you don't embrace this aspect, family values and traditions will have a greater influence, and you'll trust your own logic more.

The spiritual lineage is your higher *Self*. You may have often heard that you are not of this world. If you embrace the spiritual aspect, external factors likely have less influence on you than your own.

If you're sceptical about such matters, then why don't you have faith in yourself and everything you dream of? Are there fears, doubts, and other obstacles? This is direct evidence that the past influences you more than your current life.

Let's return to relationships. What are relationships?

"Relationships are the mutual dependence of different quantities, objects, phenomena, correlations between something." You can define the nature of any relationship; in this case, with money!

Choose as you wish, what kind of relationships are closer to you: wild, civilised, trusting, difficult, close, intimate, formal, informal.

Like any contract, relationships can be revised. The main thing is to use this rule.

What kind of relationships do you have? No, not like that! What kind of relationships would you like to have with the financial element?

If you've realised that you have relationships but they're not how you'd like them to be, or you want to revise them, remember, that's not the most important thing. The most important thing is that relationships exist! Whether they're good or bad, they exist. Something can be done with this.

If they don't exist, then there's nothing to do. There's no concept of good or bad in the financial aspect. Either they exist or they don't.

So, when they exist, you can work with them, change them, rewrite them, cancel them.

When they don't, you need to create them, and then change and remake them.

To *have* means to possess, take responsibility, care. The higher the level of responsibility, the more energy you can manage! Sometimes this doesn't relate to wealth, and there can even be a rebound effect. The more conscious a person is, the more ideal they want to see the world, themselves, their family, and friends. But nothing is ideal. Accept the fact that we're not perfect, we can make mistakes, and we're all different!

To prevent a rebound, simply allow yourself to be imperfect, but it's important to strive for the best!

When you have this *having*, you imagine how much more you can create, how much you can improve, what discoveries you can make.

In reality, wealthy people are very busy; they always lack time.

If you want to become wealthy hoping that you won't have to do anything, then, most likely, the path to your financial wealth will be long.

Practical Exercise
Defining Your Relationship with Yourself

How often do you criticise yourself?
How often do you praise yourself?
Do you finish your projects?
Do you keep your promises?
Do you raise the bar of your standard of living?
Do you accept your weaknesses?
Do you work on your mindset?
Do you study financial literacy?
Are you satisfied with your surroundings?
How many *yes* and *no* answers did you get?

CHAPTER 7

A Bit About Me

Why did I suddenly decide to tell you about all of these rules of money relationships and almost ask you to sign a blood contract?

Let's get to know each other.

You've seen my name on the cover. I'm an ordinary/unordinary person whose life has had periods of *plenty* followed by hungry days.

My parents were in the military. When military service was respected, the lives of military personnel were quite secure. Then my parents transitioned to civilian life, and our family had to learn to live anew.

Financial literacy was not a skill anyone possessed. Attempts by my parents to delve into the market business also didn't lead to success. I started working at the age of 16.

Studying and working were made possible by the discipline instilled in me by my parents since childhood. No one ever taught me how to manage money.

This marked the beginning of my long journey to self-discovery, and the challenging lessons of the *money* element began.

Like in my childhood: one moment I had plenty, the next I had little. Business attempts, one credit after another, continuous investments in myself, changing professions, working with consciousness and subconsciousness—try to find techniques I haven't explored through my own experience.

And what was the result? If there's a question, then there will be an answer! All my previous lessons, training, losses, and expenses had their impact. They instilled an unshakable belief in me! But I didn't see the financial results …

During the second wave of the pandemic, I went to the Maldives for four months, without money, and without an understanding of how to deal with debts.

I'll tell you the story of what I did there and about how the owner of the guesthouse where I worked became the president of the island in another book. Now let's return to our precious money.

One day, sitting on the shore of the Indian Ocean, where the Moon is bigger than the Sun, I realised that I had built relationships with people, with myself, with energies, with the Moon. Can you imagine? If you really want it, you can build such relationships. But I couldn't define what money was.

I had heard somewhere that money is energy and repeated those words to myself. I really didn't understand, what is this *energy*?

I associated the word *energy* with physical labour or sports. How else can you expend energy? I had never seen people earning millions with a shovel. What kind of energy is this? People earn much more sitting at a computer, expending their energy with the click of their fingers. What's the connection?

And I seriously decided to delve into the question of *what is money?*

At some point, I realised that on an island where tourists sometimes outnumbered locals, green banknotes came into my possession. I worked, and I was paid. But I didn't understand what money was. It struck me as being so funny that I almost burst into tears.

I felt something similar during a singing lesson. I write music and lyrics for songs. But I didn't like how I sang, and I took vocal lessons for several years. I was taught by a talented opera singer. One day she asked, 'Do you understand that notes have weight? Place?'

What? Notes have weight? I can't understand what notes are if I can't see or hear them.

The singer was very surprised. For her, notes were alive, but for me, they didn't exist in a material sense. For her, they were like drops; each note had its own thread, its own density, while for me, they were just a collection of sounds. Do you see the difference? That's why she is an internationally experienced singer, while I'm still learning to sing.

The same goes for money! For some, it is dense, alive, and for others, it is just pieces of paper, well, or ... an app on the phone. I started with the simplest.

In the Maldives, many people wanted a massage (I am a professional masseuse, and I indicated this in my social networks), but I didn't understand *how much to charge* for my services on an island in the Indian Ocean, so I let clients name their own price.

People were from different countries, so the amounts varied.

The most interesting part was that I didn't know where to spend these earnings. Remember that I was in debt up to my neck, and the very thought of spending money would trigger unpleasant emotions. I simply stashed my earnings away in a drawer or under the mattress. I can't remember anymore.

For me, valuable experiences were interactions with people, their feedback on my massages, and the benefits of my unique techniques. Of course, I desired financial compensation, but naming the price myself was even more difficult than explaining what money was.

People paid money, but what should I do with it? Moreover, I noticed that I was receiving less and less money, but people started giving me gifts: books, paintings, hats, once even a coffee maker.

Can you imagine? On that island, I had everything!

That's when I began to contemplate the history of the origin of money. Payment for my services was essentially an exchange.

That's an exchange I understand.

I was exchanging massage techniques, my hands, knowledge, time, and energy. And it was still equivalent to money.

The combination of all these factors adds up to a price.

I understand the concept of price as well!

And here came the pivotal moment. I set a price for my services, and what do you think happened? I lost clients? Believe it or not, I lost not a single client!

That's how your personal relationship with money affects the number of customers.

No relationship, no customers.

Another moment occurred on the island. While I was contemplating how to spend my hard-earned money, I fell ill. This rarely happens to me, and everything I had saved had to be spent on a visit to the local doctor!

I had to change my attitude towards life! You see, we even have a relationship with life!

I had to reconsider that too!

The question of how money came into existence began to torment me.

In the national British Library and from other sources, I found the following information.

Facts:

The first coins were found in Ancient Greece, China, and the Byzantine Empire around 3500 years ago.

The first cheques appeared in China in the 7th century BCE.

The word *bank* comes from the Italian *banko*—a round table, a negotiating table.

The first records of banking transactions are known from the times of the Roman Empire and the Byzantine Empire.

Even back then, there were moneylenders; money was borrowed and lent with interest. So, what has changed over these thousands of years? I will tell you: money has become accessible to everyone!

Yes, indeed, to everyone! Previously, it was mainly available to those in power.

Does the Knights Templar Order tell you something? The treasures of these Templars are shrouded in an aura of mystery, and to this day, there are beliefs that their treasure has not been found yet.

Essentially, this group of people came together and created a closed private club. In it, everyone contributed—some with gold, some with silver, some with precious gems. Everyone contributed what they could. As you can understand, these people were not poor; they were quite prestigious, with titles. Information about each member of the Order can be found in modern sources.

Tell me, what was the foundation of this club? Honest men's word? Strength? The idea? My dear and beloved, it was the idea! What a strong idea and belief it was that means the fame of this Order lives on to this day.

These Knights of the Round Table even back then understood that they couldn't afford to be without money.

It would have been their downfall. With enough money, they could protect themselves and expand.

The Templars had a rule: to achieve their goals and prosper through their own efforts! What qualities do you think these people possessed for their word to be stronger than any contract? Could anyone join them?

This idea then took on newer and newer forms. Banking *products* started to emerge, such as loans, investments, interest rates.

States emerged for financial stability and monetary regulation. For example, San Marino, Malta, Liechtenstein. Notice, wealthy people create similar ideas.

We started with an introduction to me, and we're ending with the Knights Templar Order. Who knows, maybe I was also an honorary member of this mysterious club.

I want to tell you that everything I've gathered in this book, I have practiced and am practicing myself. In the first months after returning from the Maldives, with new programs and new relationships, I started closing my financial gaps in which I had been *living* for 6 years. Now, as I write this book, I have no panic, but there is confidence in tomorrow, a few magnets, investment plans, and many different ideas. When doubts or moments of uncertainty arise, I apply my abundance formula. Then everything falls into place, motivation appears, and confusion dissipates!

Practical Exercise
Knight of the Order

Imagine yourself as a knight of the legendary Knights Templar Order.
How do you conduct yourself? What are your principles?
Write it all down on paper.
What conditions for joining the Order would you propose?

CHAPTER 8

The Beginning of Relationships or The Million-Pound Agreement?

Let's summarise.

The history of money began with the exchange of gold. When gold was the foundation, almost all services were exchanged using promissory notes, receipts, and cheques. Gold served as the guarantee, which was lent to authoritative individuals as debt, a loan, or for specific state projects.

Then, bars and receipts were replaced by coins and certificates, and notably, money was only used during the day. Here's what I found in ancient chronicles:

In this context, the word *moneta* (*moneta*) is related to the idea of warning or reminding about a standard or value. This originates from the historical association with the place where coins were minted—the temple of the goddess Juno Moneta in Ancient Rome. It is believed that this word may be connected to the function of money as a standardised means of exchange and storage of value. Thus, the word *money* is linked to the idea of warning or reminding about the standard of value that money represents.

The word *money* originates from the Middle English word *moneie*, which in turn was borrowed from the Latin *moneta* (mint), a nickname for the temple of the goddess Juno Moneta in Rome, where coins were produced. This term is also connected with the verb *monere*, meaning *to warn* or *to remind*. It is associated with the concept of *reminding* about the standard or value that money represents

The military had their own calculations, artists had theirs. Thus, the genetic code of money is encoded differently in each social class.

So, what does this have to do with energy? A good question. Think about how much energy you and the people around you have expended. What streams of energy can we control? The more we give, the more we attract.

The amount of energy we give away frees up space to receive energy that's 1.5 times greater.

And now, we arrive at our first point in financial relationships. And that is—expenses!

Again, relationships are connections, essentially, a contract!

You can create a contract with money, periodically revise it, add or remove clauses. But there are rules, and it's advisable to know them.

So, the first point of our agreement: EXPENSES

The main component of this point is your willingness to spend, pay, or give. Specifically, it's the amount you want to give or pay.

If you want to receive something, you need to be willing to give at least one-quarter of that amount.

Are you mindful of your feelings? Do you want a million? Are you willing to spend £250,000?

Of course, you can spend less than you earn, but you will have to spend anyway. It's better to agree with this rule and voluntarily spend a certain amount.

If you keep saving all the time, money will accumulate, but not for long. Unexpected expenses will arise:

For health;

Family and friends will borrow from you;

Work-related issues will arise.

If you want to have more, you'll have to pay for it. If you want to save but also have more, you'll end up with debts.

So, it's better to understand upfront how much you are counting on. You need to *dance* around that amount. You're managing the sum you're willing to give, not the sum you're going to receive. That's the whole secret.

Dream big, vocalise the desired sums to the Universe, but at the same time, realistically assess your spending level. I insist on the spending level. Also, try to measure the difference between the level you'd like to be at and where you are currently! The difference will be the amount of your expenses, I assure you.

Once you understand what you're lacking, step by step, you will rise to your desired level.

Making a big leap can make your head spin.

But if you move at your own pace, you can reach your desired height.

It's important to understand something about debts if you have them. Debts arise when you are not at your own level. The level depends on the amount of debt. The higher you are above the level at which you allow yourself to spend, the more the Universe compensates for your request in reality through debts! If you want to live like an Arab sheikh but only have enough money for rent, you're behaving like a sheikh—living a luxurious life. How long will your finances last? A day, a week? You will see a difference between your expenses and income, and significant debts will arise. This is clear, you might say. Of course, but ...

Look at how many people around you aspire to the level they are not living at. 'Well, they are trying,' you'll say. And I will tell you that this lifestyle (beyond one's means) is the reason for accumulating debts! Buy a genuine item, not a counterfeit; allow yourself to pay its real value—then I'll say you're trying, aspiring. Then the Universe won't need to balance out your efforts with debts.

Of course, you could look at this from another angle. Suppose you're so adept at spotting replicas that you can select a product closest to the original. Your manners, behaviour, and knowledge match your level of demand, and problems only arise in the financial element. In that case, it's likely that the Universe will help you reach your desired level without debts!

Conduct an Audit:

How much can you realistically afford to pay, and how much are you currently paying?

How much money remains after your payments?

List all the numbers.

Divide a sheet of paper into two halves and write down the amounts:

In one column, the value of your apartment, how much you pay for bills, monthly grocery expenses, personal expenditures on yourself, coffee with friends, etc.

And what about the second column?

Moving towards a more comfortable level, we either pay off debts or descend to our current level.

You can make an agreement for the future. Promise that if there's more profit, you'll pay more. Allow yourself more comfort and aesthetics.

Money loves to come where a path is predefined for them. When you agree to pay, money responds instantly.

I believe the *expenses* section is clear. The more you're willing to pay, the more you can expect to receive.

Resistance might arise; you may not really want to spend money. But understand, money was originally designed for this purpose. You need to work on this. This is the pain that hinders you from becoming wealthy.

There's another extreme. If you spend too much, consider how much you spend on yourself. If your personal expenses are substantial, then congratulations, you're on the right track! You've established the first point!

Point Two: MONEY MAGNET

Oh yes, spend and save—in that sequence. Even just a penny, but save!

This is the magnet that will attract those swift folks to your address.

I want to draw your attention to the fact that if you have nothing to save, what do you plan to accumulate?

If there's nothing to save, you need to reorganise your life, not by economising on basic things, but by increasing your profit, earnings, salary. I'll provide you with a formula later, which you should apply if the situation is really bad. For now, try to accept the terms of the agreement for your future life of abundance.

Money looks more often to those who have *magnets*. The more significant the magnets are in terms of sums, the better.

I don't recommend swapping points 1 and 2. If you have problems with expenses or want to create magnets first, it's probably due to greed or fears. Deal with this point. Maybe working on your fears is worth it?

Relationships are built on the law of conservation of energy: the more we give, the more we receive. This rule is valid even in the new era. First, we create or agree to an outgoing flow, and then, when we receive a larger incoming flow, we create a money magnet.

When you see your magnets growing while expenses remain the same, you'll experience feelings of joy and pride.

Remember you agreed to move to the next level? That means you can increase your expenses. As we rise to a higher level, our income level also increases. The financial flow becomes higher, and you achieve a higher status.

Money will move towards you and be attracted by your magnets more quickly.

Magnets can be on separate accounts, in piggy banks, in separate envelopes; you can have one, two, even ten. Remember the financial literacy exercise? Five points at 10%. These same points can become magnets. Set a minimum amount for each magnet, and when the sum exceeds the minimum, invest money according to the purpose of that magnet. You'll see an improvement in your quality of life, and it will become more vibrant. More opportunities will open up for you in this life.

Point Three: HONESTY

Strange, isn't it? Nothing strange about it. Honesty in relationships is the foundation. You can't imagine how many times we deceive ourselves. Yes, ourselves.

Sit down and honestly admit to yourself all the financial manipulations. Write them down on paper if you want, or record them in audio format—whichever is easier for you—from the smallest to the largest financial manipulation.

This includes miscalculations, shortcomings, small thefts, price deception, unpaid bills, services, and consultations; even moments of *freebies* are included! In short, everything related to money and you! You might not remember everything immediately. Leave yourself a reminder. As soon as a memory resurfaces, record it. This is a very important moment. Money loves honesty. As soon as you become honest with yourself, you become a favourite of money.

This point is so crucial that without it, no relationship will work. Take your time, don't be shy, and confess your *sins* to yourself!

The level of your life depends on this point no less than on the previous ones. Only when you admit and accept yourself will your ability to attract a larger sum of money increase several times over.

Point Four: RESPONSIBILITY

It begins with the decision to sow seeds of wealth every day, taking responsibility for your life and controlling cash flows.

For those already doing this, there won't be any difficulties. For those new to this, it's worth making it a daily ritual. Record your expenses and income every day! I didn't give you that practice for nothing in the beginning.

Money loves to jump around. When you write down your expenses and income, you entertain these folks, and they love having fun as much as we do.

When you meticulously detail expenses and income, you can better control cash flows without significant energy expenditure. Remember, our energy is potentially our money.

Here's one *but*: where would we be without it. The level of our energy, including free energy, is very low.

Have you ever wondered how human energy levels can be measured? In reality, there are specialised devices, quite a few of them, that show our energy is not even enough to fry an egg. So, where do we get the energy for cash flows in the millions and billions? The majority of our energy is devoted to maintaining our body and bodily needs. If you only rely on your energy, you won't earn much. It's better to generate energy simply by counting and recounting. I suggest writing down your expenses with a + sign and income with just a number.

This is the rule of the new era—everything is in a positive key.

You need to take responsibility for the sums, for adhering to your own rules. This is the correct and reliable path to abundance and success.

I'll tell you this. All your debts—that's your potential! Just imagine your debts are all paid off. The amount you pay every month becomes not an expense but a magnet, and it stays with you, understand? That will come later. Right now, it's an indicator of saving on yourself. In the worst case, it's settling karma, but it could turn into a plus if you pay off the bills.

When you practice a family budget in writing, keep records of family expenses, take responsibility for your decisions, love and respect yourself. Money loves you even more and won't leave you without its attention.

Point Five: GRATITUDE

Gratitude is a wonderful feeling and the result of our thoughts.

If you don't keep a gratitude book yet, I highly recommend it. Express gratitude for everything and everyone! Do it as if you already have it.

Yes, yes, you want money—be thankful for money! Do this every day until it becomes a habit.

Allow me to ask you: How will you behave, feel, dress when you have money? Or more accurately, when you have the amount of money you desire?

Here we are back to the first point.

Be willing to give—and it will come back to you.

Read through all the points again; write them down. What are you agreeable with, and what triggers resistance? What beliefs come up? These thoughts are likely barriers to your wealth.

If you agree with everything, set off on a good path! Make decisions, agree, and follow through.

Practical Exercise
Abundance Contract

Write down the contract's points.
Live through each point with agreement, then with disagreement. What emotions do you feel? Repeat this exercise UNTIL YOU HAVE NO EMOTIONS, only stable confidence in fulfilling the contract.
Sign the contract, date it, and set an expiration date.
Write a letter to money and a letter from money to you (in the same format as below. If you want to write your own letter, do so, but only after the provided example).
May abundance and an endless flow of money be with you!

CHAPTER 9

Invite Money into Your Life.

After signing the agreement, the first thing you can do is invite money into your new life. You can do it in writing, formally, on beautiful paper by hand—the choice is yours. Walk out ceremoniously and wish a large sum of money to every person you meet. Just sincerely wish, mentally, the amount that you would like to receive yourself, and do this for 24 people. Feel the state that will follow this action!

I can tell you, having lived in debt with enormous interest for 10 years, that I was able to build my relationship with money using the method described above. Within a year, I paid off all personal debts. I started seeing opportunities; panic and a sense of worthlessness disappeared. Believe me, life changes, and we change too, whether we want it or not. It's better to change consciously!

I really want people to be rich both spiritually and materially! In the new matrix, money is no longer something lacking but something natural. After all, we don't feel a lack of fire, metal, or ether in our lives, do we? We already have established relationships with these elements (if you have a fear of water or another element, you can work on or renew these relationships in the same way).

It's all in your minds, or rather, in your thoughts! Remember, thoughts give birth to feelings, feelings lead to actions, and actions lead to results! Be true to yourself and your principles. Everything in the Universe has laws and rules, but we are lucky because we can change, we can create! Money can be generated! You can create the amount of money you need. Just as furniture or paper comes from a tree, fire fits into a lighter, and water streams into rain, money can be materialised.

We all have the opportunity to become successful and wealthy.

There is a lot of talk and writing about the difference in mindset, but what is the real difference?

The mindset of millionaires may differ from that of ordinary people. For example, millionaires may have more self-confidence, take more risks, and think in a more goal-oriented way and strategically. They may also be more persistent and determined, and they know how to maximise opportunities. However, this does not mean that all millionaires have the same mindset, or that ordinary people cannot achieve financial success. Many successful people are also hardworking, persistent, and skilled at maximising opportunities.

In other words, the difference lies in action. While someone is thinking, someone else is taking action! Not everyone knows how to take risks. However, if you look at the actions of successful people, you will likely find many risky actions. There is a reason for the expression, 'He who does not take risks does not drink champagne.' In the new matrix, if the risk is ecologically sound, then why not go for it?

I am not encouraging you to take risks, I am encouraging you to take action.

If you want to reduce risks, study the field in which you want to take a risk. The more knowledge you have, the less fear you will experience. Analyse and gather statistics; after all, statistics are indicators that will inform you about the state of affairs and indicate the relative necessity of action. It's a tool through which you can change the course of events in the future.

Money loves analysis, graphs, and reports. Invite money into your life, understand its language, and you will be able to reach unprecedented heights.

You can track your own statistics daily. You will see how the formula changes your situation.

Waiting and simply enduring will not bring you more financial attention. You need to take action. Yes, my wonderful ones. First, manifestation, then reorganisation (or saving).

Manifestation =⟩ reorganisation =⟩ high creditworthiness =⟩ financial stability

This formula works for individuals as well as for companies. The high rate of business failures (one out of eleven experiences failure in the first year), constant bankruptcies, and government failures indicate that this knowledge is not being utilised, even if it's known.

Disappearing empires always fell into financial pits, and they couldn't handle them by relying solely on saving and management changes. However, you cannot get out of a crisis by solely relying on saving. The goal of saving is merely to ensure that expenses do not exceed income. During a crisis, this doesn't work. When saving is used as the only solution, it won't bring you back to the previous level.

Think about moving forward and emphasise it.

No empire remains in the same state. Empires either expand or shrink.

Expansion happens when there's progress =》 good administration =》 sensible saving

Expansion decreases when this order is disturbed.

Decline always comes when they start with saving—then there's nothing left to promote. The order of affairs almost never leads back to the previous state, and when saving is applied, there is nothing to preserve capital on.

Invite money! They need to know what they are coming for and what they will be spent on.

The need to earn money urgently requires brilliance in promotion. It is impossible to start promoting or manifesting too early. So, what is *too early*? Let's clarify. The less time you have, the more brilliance is required.

Therefore, your communicativeness, ability to analyse, and actions geared towards long-term results attract financial flows.

Providing services and goods is the main way to overcome emergencies and even inflation. Aim for good, honest service provision!

Invite money into your life by simply being aware of opportunities! In reality, there are many opportunities, we just aren't accustomed to noticing them. Start right now.

Practical exercise
Overcoming an Emergency Situation

Write down what you provide?
For yourself.
Taking care of your health, body, education, personal development, etc.
For your family.
Each family member contributes to the household. The work of underage children is to study and maintain cleanliness at home. Non-working grandparents can take care of grandchildren (this doesn't mean they should be full-time nannies). A family is a team where everyone works together.
For other people.
Your professional services.
Be sincere: how do you provide your work (in a broad sense)? What opportunities did you see today for attracting money? (Hint: even a clean floor affects money attraction.)

CHAPTER 10

Wealth and Success Are Normal. And Money Too.

Let's take as our foundation that wealth and success are a normal state of affairs. If it's not like that for you, there might be some pathology. To prevent it from becoming a disease, start preventive measures right now. And, of course, the most crucial ingredient is love!

If you don't love money, you don't love yourself, you don't accept yourself, and you don't acknowledge the rules of the game that you accepted a long time ago when you came into this life. Love for people is the recognition of your talents within yourself. Everything around us is a reflection of our thoughts!

You and only you are the cause of everything you have and don't have. Let's acknowledge our responsibility for our lives, take everything into our own hands, and start giving tasks to our minds instead of obeying incorrect beliefs.

Our mind is our assistant. It seeks ways to fulfil our desires. Love comes from within us!

Even debts are our manifestation. Be thankful, accept, and give back. Debt is a confirmation of your strength; free yourself from confinement and enjoy freedom.

We love and acknowledge the new stage, the new matrix, and the new life. We reclaim our right to abundance, to live in plenty. It's natural and normal.

Admit your love to yourself! You are energy and power. You don't need to ask for anything; you just need to love. Love yourself, love life, love money. Money is an element of the new era, the right to abundance, a condition of the game called *life*. So, let's acknowledge love more often.

I can understand moments of anger and indignation. Let me explain. If money is associated with greed or violence, with something negative and deadly, it's normal not to love it. But why should all of the above be considered *normal*? And why should it be associated with money?

Money doesn't change people, it shows who people really are! Greed is not a definition of money, it's a character trait of a person. And, by the way, you won't get far with greed. Remember the famous global financial crisis of 2008? Remember Madoff? Mavrodi? The most famous financial pyramids that caused many people to lose millions of their savings. It was the longest-lasting adventure built on human greed. People wanted to do nothing and receive large interest rates. Tell me, who will pay you money for simply voluntarily giving away your hard-earned money? Just like that, without your involvement, without your time, and without your energy. Can you personally come up with something for which such commissions could be paid?

If you have such an idea, please do let me know; I'll personally pay you for it. I love brilliant ideas. I love self-confident people, and even those who acknowledge their greed and avarice because only an honest person acknowledges their dark side. Only a person who knows themselves, a responsible person, can be truly honest.

Not long ago, I realised that money is a reflection of a free soul that not only accepts the rules of the game but also creates them. How can you not love that!

So, my dear ones, if you don't know how much love you need for a complete and happy life, sit down and calculate how much money you need to survive. It's much easier than complaining about what you lack. I advise you to forget such phrases as: 'We are poor, we can't afford it' or 'We don't have money.' Simply eradicate such words from your vocabulary. Dream about Great Love. Plan your own wealth, and then you'll see immense reserves.

Never create obstacles, spaces, time. You must ensure that you, your family members (and your employees) are very, very, very busy.

Some people are accustomed to spending everything they earn. This is as foolish as striving to earn only enough to cover expenses. You must have reserves. If you have them, consider them and exchange them for cash.

If you encounter a financial problem, don't panic and don't come up with strange, unusual solutions. Usually, we get into trouble because we don't stick to our usual actions! Doing something even more unusual is a huge mistake.

Promote yourself, your services, your talents, your skills. This is the shortest path to earning money.

Your love for people is your creditworthiness. Even if you have no savings, but you have high creditworthiness, many doors will open for you. Your company will be welcomed, and you may have as many opportunities as those with overflowing savings.

I'll emphasise again that arguments like 'we are poor' or 'we are in an extreme financial situation' used to find explanations for unpaid bills, completely contradicting the formula:

Promote =⟩ Change (the way you act) =⟩ Save =⟩ Provide

Complaining about poverty violates this formula, not to mention programming your bleak future.

If you execute the steps in the wrong sequence (for example, saving at the expense of promotion), the existence of your entire company (project, family, personal financial future) will be at risk. Actions for promotion in your financial sphere during a downturn involve maintaining confidence in your company's creditworthiness, presenting things in the best light, and motivating employees to earn more money for the company. You are as rich as you promote, provide, and sensibly handle your money. Strengthen creditworthiness in emergency situations. These are actions for promotion.

Practical Exercise
Letter to Money

Rewrite the letter below in your own name, and then, if you wish, write your letter.

Hello, my dear, I am very excited about our new relationship based on trust, abundance, principles, and mutual love. I have been looking forward to our cooperation, and I am ready for our long-term contract.

You will be safe and secure with me! You can grow, circulate, and stay in my accounts throughout my life. I will release you for purchases and joyfully await your return in double or even triple the amount.

Together, we will enjoy luxurious, high-quality, and comfortable things. So be it!

Try writing yourself a letter from the perspective of money and see what comes up.

CHAPTER 11

Old and New Rules!

Let's consider a few more rules of the bygone era and see how they have been transformed in the new age.

'You can't buy happiness with money, but you can rent it.'

Tell me, how can one spend money on happiness? We have the right to both money and happiness. These are not mutually exclusive concepts, they complement each other. Happiness is an internal state, while money is external. Why trade one for the other?

'If you want to be happy, be happy; if you want to be rich, be rich.'

Respecting the material side of life in this world gives you the chance to explore its spiritual aspects. Your well-being depends on your own decisions. Have you noticed that creating, acting, and being specific can be challenging? So what will help you move forward? Incorporate dates and numbers (i.e., concrete figures) into your thought process, and you will see progress and start moving.

Once you agree to have a relationship with money, implement the rules of financial literacy and planning. The results won't make you wait!

What does it mean to *be rich*? (If we talk about finances.)

'Your well-being depends on your own decisions,' said John D. Rockefeller. And this is true to this day. Add numbers to your desires, and you will get results much faster. Put dates in any plan, numbers in any account, and expenses with a + sign in any report. Create wealth for yourself.

And how about this statement: *Work as if money doesn't matter!*

In the new relationships, this rule does not work at all, not at all!

Everything matters: your work and your money! The longer and more you create something, the more valuable it becomes! You can philosophise and ponder about goals, meanings, callings, but, in the end, it all comes down to a certain number. Therefore, everything matters.

Don't attach too much importance, but don't devalue anything either.

'Never confuse your pay check with your talent.' Think about this phrase by actor Marlon Brando. How many underrated people are there in their art and profession, and who is to blame for that? People treat us the way we allow them to, including money.

You can dig into your subconscious for a lifetime, searching for reasons. It's useful and necessary, but I suggest another option.

What was, was. Embrace the new era. Set new rules and create a new life.

Money is neither good nor evil! Money is an integral part of our lives! It's better to accept it with love. But, as with everything in our world, nothing falls from the sky. You know, that's absolutely right. Just imagine if gold or bundles of money fell from the sky. I think that would be a shock.

Everything is as it should be. Start accepting reality and live in the present.

Build a relationship with this new element! If you want more money in your bank account, love money! Love life! Energy generates movement. If you build the entire chain, it looks like this:

Energy – thoughts – emotions – feelings – actions – numbers

The more positivity in your energy, the more positivity in the whole chain.

Love is the best source.

Conclusion

So, what am I talking about?

I'm talking about the fact that if we don't understand something, it doesn't mean we can't have it. When there is understanding, having things becomes much easier. And when it comes from abundance, inner self-sufficiency, and confidence, everything will eventually come to fruition.

And our beloved money needs to be managed! We need to know how to spend, but also how to save.

I really like the rule of two coffees, which my beloved recently told me about: 'The first time, treat someone to coffee out of your generosity. The second time, do it as friends. But if you pay for coffee a third time, it's out of your foolishness.' What does it mean? If someone doesn't treat you in return, don't keep treating them, otherwise, the person will take advantage of your kindness, and in the end, no one will be happy; only disappointment will remain. I use this rule in my everyday life. Knowing how to say 'no' is also an expression of love, just like saying 'yes'! In the past, I used to treat others without limits. Now, I allow myself to be treated by others.

After returning from the Maldives, I decided to follow the rules of the money contract. I started two journals: a personal one for expenses and income, where I wrote gratitude and affirmations, and a second one for business. Every week, I analysed various aspects, such as whether I was doing fair exchanges, whether I had enough money on the magnet, whether I set goals correctly, and so on. I started hiring mentors and coaches. The results were astonishing!

I became complacent and stopped maintaining the journals. And guess what? As soon as I relaxed, my progress declined. I got scared. Do I have to start all over again? Are my efforts and rules all meaningless, just illusions?

Starting from the new year, I restored the journaling tradition, and in three months, I regained the results!

The journal and the contract are what I brought back to London. That's where my journey to money began.

Love makes you move forward; love inspires. And when you can see all of that in the form of money, in numbers, love grows, doesn't it? How much can you achieve in life when you have an element such as MONEY in your hands?

I've shared a real story with you. Relationships can and should be reevaluated, contracts rewritten, agreements made on terms that suit you! The Universe loves everyone, and we need to love the Universe within ourselves. And create, create, create.

The author

Meet Angelica Fomina, an author whose passion for self-improvement and personal growth has led to the creation of inspiring and educational books. Born in Lithuania, Angelica embarked on a long journey to find herself and her true purpose. Seven years spent in the fertile lands of Ukraine and twenty years in the dynamic atmosphere of London have allowed her to accumulate a wealth of experience and knowledge. In her book "From Fear to Love", Angelica shares her personal achievements and practical advice, helping readers transform their relationship with money and achieve financial well-being. Her works serve as a realistic guide to positive change, and she eagerly shares her insights to inspire others on their path to success. Get ready for an exciting journey of self-discovery and success with Angelica Fomina!

novum PUBLISHER FOR NEW AUTHORS

The publisher

„ **He who stops
getting better
stops being good.**

This is the motto of novum publishing, and our focus is on finding new manuscripts, publishing them and offering long-term support to the authors.
Our publishing house was founded in 1997, and since then it has become THE expert for new authors and has won numerous awards.

Our editorial team will peruse each manuscript within a few weeks free of charge and without obligation.

You will find more information about
novum publishing and our books on the internet:

www.novum-publishing.co.uk